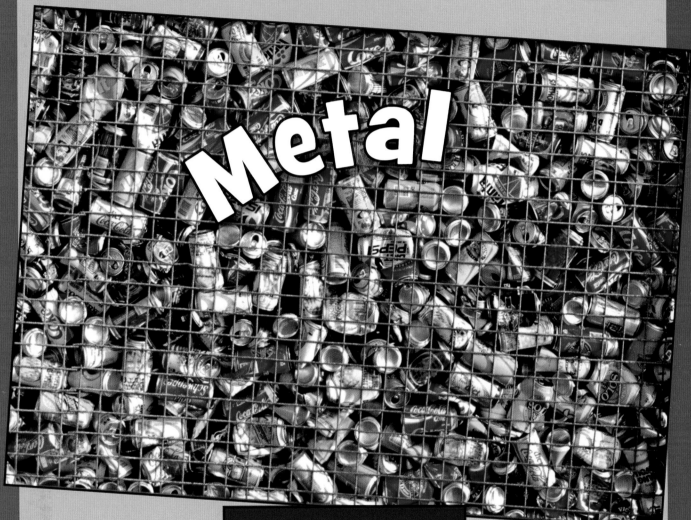

Metal

Dana Meachen Rau

mc Marshall Cavendish
Benchmark
New York

To the students of JFK Elementary School, Windsor, Connecticut
—D.M.R.

With thanks to Professor Keith Sheppard, Department of Chemical Engineering & Materials Science, Stevens Institute of Technology, Hoboken, New Jersey, for the careful review of this manuscript

Editor: Christina Gardeski
Publisher: Michelle Bisson
Art Director: Anahid Hamparian
Series Designer: Virginia Pope

Printed in Malaysia
1 3 5 6 4 2

Library of Congress Cataloging-in-Publication Data
Rau, Dana Meachen, 1971–
Metal / Dana Meachen Rau.
pages cm. — (Use It! Reuse It!)
Includes bibliographical references and index.
Summary: "Examines how we use metal in everyday objects, its unique traits and qualities, and how it is processed to be useful to us. Also discusses how metal can be recycled to use again"—Provided by publisher.
ISBN 978-1-60870-516-0 (print)
ISBN 978-1-60870-772-0 (ebook)
1. Metals—Juvenile literature. I. Title.
TA459.R38 2011
620.1'6--dc22
2010050198

Photo research by Connie Gardner

Cover photo by Stockbroker/Superstock

The photographs in this book are used by permission and through the courtesy of: *Superstock*: pp. 1, 13, 19(T), 21(TR) Stockbroker; pp. 4(L), 8(L), 14(L), 18(L) age fotostock; p. 6(TL) F1 Online; p. 6(B) Food and Drink; p. 15 image broker; p. 17(B) Science Faction; p. 18 Vision of America. *PhotoEdit*: p. 21(TL) Kayte Deioma. *Getty Images*: p. 3 Allan Shoemake; p. 4 John Zoiner; p. 5(T) Roger T. Schmidt; p. 5(B) Sean Justice; p. 14 Phil Degginger; p. 16(T) Michael Rosenfeld; p. 16(C) David Aschkenas; p. 16(B) Bloomberg; p. 21(B) Tim MacPherson. *Corbis*: p. 6(TR) Brian Summers; pp. 7(B), 12(R) Corbis News; p. 20(T) Surf. *Alamy*: p. 17(T) Caro. *The Image Works*: p. 7(T) Gloria Wright; p. 19(B) Alex Fainsworth. *Art Resource*: pp. 8, 9 Erich Lessing; p. 10 The Trustees of The British Museum; p. 12(L) SSPL National Media Museum. *AP Photo*: p. 11(L). *Granger Collection*: p. 11(R).

Metal

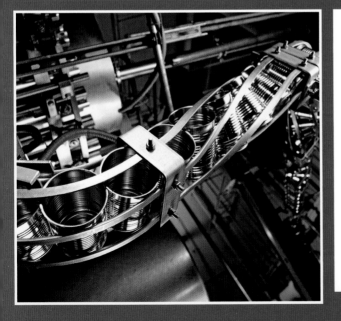

Chapter 1

Clear the runway!
Here comes a plane
made of metal.

Made of Metal

Here's a riddle. What do you play with, eat with, travel in, live in, and even wear? It's metal!

Most metals are shiny. That makes them a good material for jewelry, like rings and necklaces. Metals also withstand heat. That's why cookie sheets are made of metal. Electricity can run through metal easily. So the wires in your house are made of this material.

Metal is strong. It's used to make streetlights and machines, such as computers and refrigerators.

Silver is used to make jewelry.

Use oven mitts when you take a cookie tray out of the oven. The metal gets hot!

A motorcycle is made of metal. So are many kitchen tools.

It's used for parts of **vehicles**, like bikes, cars, boats, and planes.

Check the toolbox. Hammers, screwdrivers, and other tools are made of metal. So are kitchen tools, like forks, spoons, measuring cups, and aluminum foil. Metal cans hold cat food, tomato sauce, and vegetables. Soda and other **beverages** also come in cans.

Metal can be melted and then molded into shapes—like a paper clip

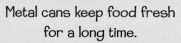

Metal cans keep food fresh for a long time.

or trumpet. Bits of metal are also found in medicines, paint, and makeup. Copper, gold, iron, lead, silver, tin, and aluminum are just some of the metals we use every day.

Metal makes music, too!

Your home, planet Earth, is made of metal. Earth has a very hot iron center. Closer to the surface, you can find rocks that contain metals. These rocks are called **ores**. Metal makes up many things around you.

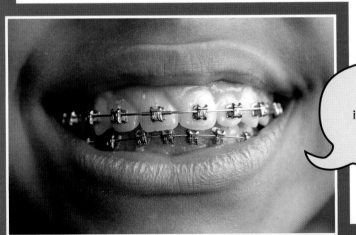

You have metal in your mouth if you have braces.

Chapter 2

More than 4,000 years ago, people crafted this axe head from copper.

8

Metal through the Ages

Ancient people used natural materials to make tools, weapons, and decorations. If they lived near the shore, they might use shells. If they lived in the forest, they used wood and rock. Early people discovered metals, too.

As far back as 9,000 years ago, copper was one of the first metals used for tools and weapons. Copper, and some other metals, are soft enough to hammer into different shapes.

People found that metal could also be melted. When metal got very hot, it turned **molten**. This liquid metal

People long ago found many uses for copper because it was soft and easy to shape.

could be poured into a **mold**. When the metal cooled, it turned hard again. So people could mold it into arrowheads, bracelets, or any shape they needed.

People also discovered they could mix metals together to make them stronger. Mixtures of metals are called **alloys**. Bronze is an alloy of copper and tin. It became the main material to make spears, knives, shields, and swords in many ancient civilizations.

Iron, one of the most common metals on Earth, was hard to melt. It needed very high temperatures. But about 3,000 years ago, people built

Metal was a good material for weapons, such as this shield from more than 2,000 years ago.

A furnace heats metal to make it soft.

Then it can be hammered or molded into different shapes.

furnaces and developed ways to make iron usable. They heated it and hammered it into shape. They melted it and poured it into molds.

Many communities had a blacksmith. He made lots of everyday items, such as nails, door hinges, bells, and horseshoes. Iron helped farming by giving farmers stronger and better equipment to use. Iron was used to make weapons, like guns. Buildings and bridges could be made stronger and last longer than ever before.

The use of metal reached new heights when it was used to build skyscrapers.

Metal makes up the framework, and many other parts, of a car.

The alloy steel was discovered thousands of years ago, but was not widely used until the 1850s. Steel is a mix of iron and another substance called carbon. People found that steel was much stronger than iron. They used it to make railroad tracks, bridges, cars, and skyscrapers. Steel is the most common metal that we use today.

There are lots of other metals on Earth. Many were not discovered until after 1800. One of these was aluminum. People started using aluminum to make soda cans in the 1960s. Before that, soda came in glass bottles. Today, soda cans are still one of aluminum's main uses.

Aluminum is lighter than steel, so it is used to make airplanes. It also does not **corrode** as much as steel. When steel corrodes, it gets rusty.

Gold is a very valuable metal. It is the only metal that does not corrode in nature. It can also be shaped by hammering or melting and molding. That's why people make jewelry out of gold.

Gold has always been a sign of wealth because it is so expensive and beautiful.

13

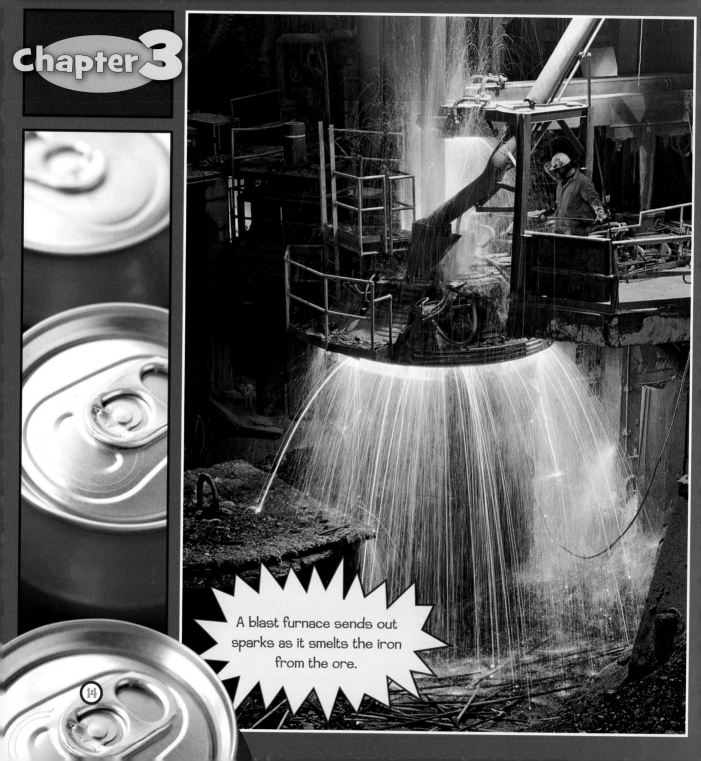

Chapter 3

A blast furnace sends out sparks as it smelts the iron from the ore.

Melting and Molding

We use the metals iron and aluminum to make many products. The metals start underground as ores. **Miners** dig, chip, and blast rock to collect the ores.

Next, the metal has to be **smelted** from the ore. Smelting means removing the metal from the rock. Metalworkers use **chemicals**, heat, and electricity to take out aluminum. To smelt iron, the ore is sent to a blast furnace. The ore, **coke**, and other ingredients are heated together with blasts of hot air. Coke is a fuel that burns and gives off heat. The iron turns to liquid.

Molten metals may go to another furnace to be combined with **scrap metal** and other ingredients to make an alloy. Most iron is made into the alloy steel.

Miners drill ore out of rock.

The liquid metal is poured into a mold and cooled into the mold's shape. This is usually a long slab, but it can be a shape called an **ingot**. Slabs and ingots are sent to **foundries** where they will be made into products people can use.

At the foundry, the steel is melted and poured into molds. Sand is sometimes used for molds. After the metal cools, the sand is broken away from the final piece. Instead of melting, slabs can be made into long bars for railway tracks and beams for buildings. Slabs and ingots can also be squeezed by rollers into flat sheets. Steel sheets can be stamped into molds to make car bodies.

Hot, molten metal is poured into molds at a foundry.

A large steel slab is cut into smaller pieces.

Metal is made into many products—from large washing machines to tiny screws.

Aluminum sheets are made into soda cans. A machine cuts a circle out of the sheet and then presses it into a deep cup shape to make the body of the can. A flat aluminum top is added to finish the can. The can is trimmed, cleaned, and printed with the name of the soda. Then it is sent to a beverage company to be filled. Besides cans, aluminum is also used to make siding for houses, parts for cars, and aluminum foil.

Soda cans are one of aluminum's main uses.

These cans wait in a warehouse to be filled with soda.

17

Chapter 4

Metal needs to be separated into different types at a recycling center.

Reusing Metal

Do you throw all of your trash in the garbage can? Or do you check to see if something can be recycled first? Metal can be recycled. In fact, many metal items that you use are made from metal that has been used before. Scrap metal is an important ingredient in new metal products.

Scrap metal can come from old cars, old appliances, or other metal products. You can help recycle smaller pieces of metal. Some towns and cities pick up your **recyclables**. In other communities, you may have to bring your recyclables to a center yourself.

The metal from old cars and appliances can be used again.

19

Steel cans and aluminum cans are easy to recycle.

At the recycling center, the metal is sorted by type. A magnet pulls out cans made of steel. Electricity may be used to separate the aluminum. Machines crush the metal into **bales**. These bundles of metal can be sold back to companies to melt down and make into new products.

Recycling helps the Earth reuse its metals. If we don't recycle metal, the Earth may run out! There is only so much metal ore that people can mine and turn into products.

Before you toss a can into the recycling bin, be sure to rinse it well.

A machine crushes metal into easy-to-ship bales.

CASH FOR CANS

If your local recycling center doesn't accept some metal items, think of ways you can recycle them yourself.

You may be able to bring aluminum cans back to your local grocery store. In some states, the store pays you money for them. Then you can use those metal coins in your pocket to buy something special!

In some states, you can trade in aluminum cans for money. You're helping reuse metal, and making money for yourself, too!

21

Glossary

alloys [AL-ois] mixtures of metals

bales [BAILS] compressed bundles of material

beverages [BEV-er-ij-es] drinks

chemicals [KEM-i-kuhls] substances found in the earth or created by mixing, heating, or changing them

coke [KOHK] a fuel made from coal that contains a lot of carbon

corrode [kur-ROHD] to wear away from a chemical reaction

foundries [FOWN-dreez] places where molten metal is molded into shapes

furnaces [FUR-nis-iz] devices that create a lot of heat

ingot [ING-guht] a bar of metal

miners [MY-ners] workers who dig in the ground for metals or other natural resources

mold [MOHLD] a hollow form used to make an object by filling it with a material that takes the shape of the form

molten [MOHL-ten] turned into a liquid state by heating

ores [ORS] rocks that contain metal

recyclables [ree-SAHY-kluh-buhls] items that can be made into products again

scrap metal [SKRAP MET-l] metal that has been used before

smelted [SMELT-ed] the way metal is removed from its ore

vehicles [VEE-i-kuhls] devices that bring people from one place to another

Books to Discover

Fix, Alexandra. *Reduce, Reuse, Recycle: Metal*. Chicago, IL: Heinemann Library, 2007.

George, Lynn. *What Do You Know about the Gold Rush?* New York: PowerKids Press, 2008.

Inches, Alison. *The Adventures of an Aluminum Can: A Story about Recycling*. New York: Little Simon, 2009.

Langley, Andrew. *Everyday Materials: Metal*. NY: Crabtree Publishing, 2008.

Plomer, Anna Llimós. *Let's Create: Metal*. Milwaukee, WI: Gareth Stevens Publishing, 2004.

Websites to Explore

Chem4Kids: Metal Basics
www.chem4kids.com/files/elem_metal.html

Earth 911: Metal
http://earth911.com/recycling/metal

4 2 Explore: Mining
http://42explore.com/mining.htm

Kids Science Experiments: Magnetic Materials
www.kids-science-experiments.com/magneticmaterialfacts.html

23

Index

About the Author

Dana Meachen Rau is the author of more than 250 books for children. She has written about many nonfiction topics from her home office in Burlington, Connecticut. The metal items Dana uses most every day are a spoon to stir her cocoa, scissors to make crafts, and paper clips to hold her papers together!

With thanks to the Reading Consultants:

Nanci R. Vargus, Ed.D., is an Assistant Professor of Elementary Education at the University of Indianapolis.

Beth Walker Gambro is an Adjunct Professor at the University of Saint Francis in Joliet, Illinois.